Brumal Stillness

Michael Martinez

Brumal Stillness
by Michael Martinez

Copyright 2020 Michael Martinez
All Rights Reserved

ISBN 978-1-7337939-5-7
Published by Michael Martinez
PO Box 64324, Sunnyvale CA 94088

mwtzzz@gmail.com

Printed on demand starting 07/2020

twelve monkeys are typing the story of mankind
it starts with a ruse
and ends with a rhyme

tree branches
on a still golden sky
move with the wind
directing your gaze
to a point in the overworld
where the destiny
of each member of mankind
is wrought
from the hue that can blend
all color into one

and draw the shape of green tree
branches
on the infinite motionless palette.
draw the shape of steel
and the shape of trees
the pale canvas
and the nameless form

transcendental destiny
the destiny of man
wrought from the hue
can blend all color into one

all objects burst into being
on the infinite motionless palette
the act of contrast
the act of existence
the forming of discernment
primordial refusal
refusal to dissipate

draw the shape of steel

and the shape of trees
two things exist:
the pale canvas
and propped against it
the nameless form

in the tranquil night
I say goodnight
to you moon
casting your pure white light

across fields of alfalfa
come distant soothing sounds
and the rising sweet scent tonight

I lie by myself
snug under covers
alone in my room
in the nighttime world

a faraway dog barks
across alfalfa fields
a highway truck makes
its solitary way

Good night, moon

faraway fantasy lands
hypnotize me with soothing sounds
alone in my room

a highway that takes one
under moons and stars
far away
to a future vague

under the starry landscape
and the desert air

from solitude
to love, I hope

love is elusive
it may remain
forever unattained

among the outline
of jagged-topped mesas
among the scattered sagebrush
in a moonlit negative

the highway one day
will take me faraway
to a future unknown
to a future vague

(Grey Skies and Blue Waters)

a question still sometimes appears
even after all these years

in the midst of a mundane situation
you shook it up in justified indignation
I felt my interest piqued
a resonant chord was plucked
a melody with promising characteristic

You proposed a hike
in the warm sun
Where I bathed in
your youthful spirit

You proposed a hike
up enchanting rock
where I basked in
your self assurance

the sun beat my brain
my heart, my poor timorous heart
fluttered more
wish-wired and quiet

my heart, my poor timorous heart
fluttered more
the hint of a vast world

an expression on your face almost unnoticed
a sudden unobtrusive pensive streak

your Michigan grey skies
brooding now
invading our Texas sun

beneath your girlish charms
dark clouds have swelled
and a deeper current flows

so many questions
I couldn't ask
so much desire
i couldn't express

you are an oasis in the desert
grey skies and blue waters

Your grey skies and blue waters
(I wanted to tell you)
Your grey skies and blue waters
(an idyllic afternoon)
Your grey skies and blue waters
(sun-bleached and spotless)
Your grey skies and blue waters
(I feel slow and sluggish)

Your past is a mystery to me
I too am running far away

Blurred under the desert sun
Trying to escape the shifting sands
Freezing when the words come too fast

We find ourselves by chance together

at this juncture in this transfer station

there is a glimmer of distant comfort
shimmering at the far end platform

Can we make it ourselves intact
through the noise, the maddening crowd
past the sounds and the fury now
past the bosch garden triptych

Your grey skies and blue waters
(I wanted to tell you)
Your grey skies and blue waters
(an idyllic afternoon)
Your grey skies and blue waters
(sun-bleached and spotless)
Your grey skies and blue waters
(I feel slow and sluggish now)

Your blonde hair enveloping me
like a cradle in a rocking ocean

like a cradle in a rocking ocean
we find ourselves drowning now

in the turbulent waters of youth

drifting in these murky waters
I want you to tell me now
the dolphin tattoo
on your ivory ankle
the dophin tattoo
on your ivory ankle

in light blue
no closer to
the lighthouse in blue
no closer to
it ended much too soon

Your gentle smile and soft demeanor
humble me
your cool gaze
humbles me

Seventy with the windows
melt into the picture
thinking about forever, now
Seventy with the windows
you and me on time is
Plow for our tomorrows, yeah

Too late ... It's never late, is now
Too late ... It's never late, is now

We can't do much better
someday in our real lives
we will really live them, yeah
Somehow we are still now
try to be alive now
Strive for some unknown thing, yeah

Too late ... It's never late, is now
Too late ... It's never late, is now

it was a glorious summer
of long hours in the park
of politics and philosophy and girls

At first I almost dismissed you
your sheepish grin

your government way of talking

i'm glad i didn't
i was naive and hungry to learn

a summer i'll never forget
you leaning back in your chair
gazing at the sky behind dark glasses

stories

a story of a long battle between two birds
above the plains in Africa

stories

of meetings with people in power
of suprise and secret messages
tense moments
deception

you
now half shattered
shaky hands
half broken spirit
the weight of heavy burden

beyond any normal reckoning

but still a commanding presence
the power
the penetrating eyes
the piercing thought

Dreaming in the Rockies
reaching the depths of primality
an azure sunset
the golden finger of Being

It's beginning to rain outside
the thunder rumbles
I take a minute to reflect

what the world has in store
for me in years to come
will I find love

I'm looking for a gentle love
simple, fun, quiet

Gentle love like gentle rain

Gentle love like music
an end in sight
but the harmony doesn't want to get there

to live and not stray too far on a discordant path

A love that is soft
not loud

A love that is mellow
not rough

A love that concludes on the natural key

Every day it was in my thoughtss
Every day I prepared a little more

imagining how you'd like it
imagining how it'd bring you joy

I'm waiting for any little sign
Any sign that things will be alright

Is this how it's gonna be
Are you playing games with me

a picture perfect portrait of repose
a never ending set of tomorrows
I know
I know
I know

the air is charged with a rare electric scent
in my mind we are molding clay from earth

Is it too early has the dawn not broken yet
I can't wait I feel we're wasting time

you aren't responding anymore do I give up
tell me what to do i can't do this alone

the silent passages in the halls of time
echo in the chambers

A picture perfect portrait of repose
A never ending set of tomorrows

Clear blue skies and clear blue waters
giving space where space is due

I still hide
behind shyness of heart
I freeze
when the words come too fast
I seek
tenderness of spirit

I still long
for a gentle touch
A walk in the park
is the perfect date
an evening stroll around the city square

The simple things are best
the park is lovely at this time of year
drop by for a cup of tea
unannounced and always welcome

Let's go window shopping on fifth avenue
Let's sit on a bench and watch
everyone else

Take a stroll through the apple orchards of our youth
Daisies running riot in the golden twilight.

I still hide in starry skies
with tears of brumal stillness.
Moving in a translucent world.

I still hide in earnest sorrow for our ephemeral lives.
Bridge is reaching to you from across forever.

Let's take it in slow

Let's not venture far from simple kindness

From anonymity you were called
and relunctantly you went.

Living with the memories in the twilight of your life
the pain, betrayal and chastisement
as strong as ever
you say to anyone who will listen:

the hot desert sun
the carrion birds
the smell of death
no more to follow

The King is dead.
The land is scorched
stained red
the people are parched.

The artillery echoes across the plain.
The people cannot cry.

living in symbols
can't see the truth
forever consigned
to moving in mists

hidden beneath us
just beyond reach
since the foundation of the world

the truth would destroy us
it's a zero sum game
animal conscious works in mysterious ways

original veil forged
in brumal stillness
drifting amidst us throughout the ages

from the dim smoky flicker
of the first night time fire
there is a blind spot in our vision

to the erudite light
of the democratic age
there is a hazy poetic distraction

constructing laws from veils
we have been walking asleep
for a thousand ages

we wonder
is Cosette lost to history
among the cyclic epochs of men

the past is still here
the smoky confusion
when our thoughts and our dreams drift together

we follow the outline of the lituus in the sky
the cinerary urn behind us in shadow

ignoring the sword leaning on the fasces
we read the language of our time

discoursing within the labyrinth of custom
is there no balance to be had
on the human scale

this is the forever lament
we know not why we do
this is the forever lament

this is the forever lament
we know not what we do
this is the forever lament

This thing it always comes between us
it's a thorn in my side
it consumes my waking moments
and returns to haunt my dreams

You want more than love
I need love more than anything

Moments we giggle and throw tiger somersaults
your smile precious as I toss you high

tiger somersaults in the air

in the thickets you'll find a pot of honey
in the dresser drawer a bracelet of dark stones
on the mantle a small bear
in unchanging repose
observing with his mysterious dark eyes

You leave me in a broken state
short term memory
just a plaything

You taunt me
do you care
don't you care

some things are just a different matter
you say mine are too
I don't know what we can do

We leave eachother
We return again

Looking to possess our quarter love
like an alchemist turning half love
ever and always hopeful
ever and always knowing it's futile

Moments we giggle and throw tiger somersaults
your smile precious as I toss you high
tiger somersaults in the air

in the thickets you'll find a pot of honey
in the dresser drawer a bracelet of dark stones
on the mantle in unchanging repose
a small bear observing with his mysterious dark eyes

a hip bar
concrete floors and modern art
the figures in the paintings speak

we found ourselves
on one of the strategically places sofas
they went so well with the dim lights
and the reticent bartender

You told me the story
of your cab fare incident
in that third world country

we walked to a cafe
and ordered food
you teased me with stories
giving me sly looks
and sultry laughs
pitched to erotic notes

the gypsy with the nose ring
took our order

suddenly the whole scene changed
your attention was gone
ADHD Century 21
I'm hardly there

(the Imitation Culture)

surrounded by yuppies
it's all who you know and who they know and what they said

and oh my god
just give me a break
I'll show you
what it's like to be real

what do you think

imitation culture

if you're not a superstar you're nothing

American Idol
or you don't mean shit

the standard of hypocrisy
self worth by association

and what do you do?
do you create something yourself

She wakes in the morning
her apartment is small and neat

She works in an office
opportunists and sharks

making easy conversation
young and cute

Her hair is soft and shiny
her eyes are dark and pretty
her conversation is funny and light

the culture of vapid effigy
drinking beers and margaritas after work
the air sexy and sweet
the lights are low
She's not thinking
if she ever did

gossip and surface appearances
tight black pants
and a blouse that's low

her boss hits on her
she likes it

some people are nervous
some people are ugly
some people are stoned

they all wonder what it's like to nail her

most people only get a cursory glance
she's drawn to the smooth talker
the bull shitter
the guy with the fake power
and shallow thoughts

Tonight she goes home to change her clothes
and out to a bar

just this side of nothingness
coming through the black starry sky
an unceasing hammer strikes a concrete foundation

snug in my hammock
listening to faraway busy sounds
coming through the gentle blowing wind

a star is a white pinhole
which the other side
is spontaneous combustion

snug in my hammock
contemplating secret things

good nature
and concessions
and a lot of patience
shared feelings of an endless horizon of beauty
for the length of our lives

that is our youth

but it does not last

tragedy struck
at a young age
and therein the remaining course of your life
was set

you've become a hermit
one stage at a time

a virgin, never kissed

you and your strange ideas
you don't wear shoes they're bad for your back

but i remember previous times
weird science in your basement as kids
unbounded energy

whatever happened to the promise of your youth
the space age dreams

we know the reason why
long ago something happened
and it was too much

if you'd listen

i could tell you about
cold and clear sounds on a distant highway
thin paisley curtains against the crash of lightning

sleepless nights
freezing blankets
rain drenched leather
the quiet desert
purple mountains

suffering and bondage
summer canoes

lions and tigers on the train to vegas
midnight performances

the bridge across forever
the sterile cuckoo

the burning heart
the wild desire
the heart of loneliness
the solitary hunter

the chink in the armor
the tarnish on the brass

golden spoons chiming in a hidden chamber

the stark outline of vast lampposts
the silhouette of a black and white world

the ice man coming

the nighttime fantasies
of a solitary childhood
amidst alfalfa fields

papers falling
oil on canvas
tears on the mantlepiece

the golden twilight on endless shores
world without end

slums

there is no want of dreams

dreams are real
but promises are hollow

I sat on the park bench
in the afternoon
I watched as you walked towards me
your eyes in a thoughtful mood
your thoughts are as beautiful
as the streaming sunlight

I relish every moment now

pouring down like honey
golden sunlight in this still-frame lens

an old man strolling with a walking cane
is lost in rapture
the propietor of the Basket Shop
leans in her doorway

There is no past or future
eternity is frozen

You are the subject of this impressionist painting
content to watch you as you are

I don't need to ask you why
You'll love me forever
There is no reason why
You'll love me forever

What need is there to heal a man
if God has established
his earthly end has arrived

the day has come for you to cry
but tears do not comfort

a man's life is ignorance
punctuated by reality in tears
tears
remain with you like a tattoo

you are not yourself, then
you don't know who you are

(Mu)
Nothingness
written on their tomb
plain for you to see
Ozu and his mother
dust into the earth

to decry fate
the bond of the womb
did not go gentle into the night

to resign to fate
all for naught
eternity does not fit into now

your ashes will lie gentle
for short duration

there's lots of noise

it's time to pay attention to
the silence in music
silence in words
silence in action

www.ingramcontent.com/pod-product-compliance
Lightning Source LLC
Chambersburg PA
CBHW020954030426
42339CB00004B/90